# YOU DON'T HAVE TO BE MAD TO WORK HERE...

# YOU DON'T HAVE TO BE MAD TO WORK HERE...

Programmed by Roger Kilroy
Draughtsmanship by Ed McLachlan

**Fontana/Collins**

DAILY NEWS

PASTE SNIFFING EPIDEMIC

First published in 1982 by J.M. Dent & Sons Ltd.

This edition published in 1995 by
Chancellor Press
an imprint of Reed International Books Ltd
Michelin House
81 Fulham Road
London SW3 6RB
and Auckland, Melbourne, Singapore and Toronto

ISBN 1 85152 678 1

A CIP catalogue record for this book is available from
the British Library

Printed and bound in Great Britain
by Cox & Wyman Ltd, Reading, Berkshire

TO NOAH
The only man in history
who has been able to
float a limited company
when the rest of the world
was going into liquidation.

# WELCOME

Painkillers can ruin your life – if you're a masochist.
This book should save yours – if you've got a job and
want to survive. It's a unique 'How to ...' book that
tells you everything you every wanted to know about life
at work but were too afraid/apathetic/inebriated to ask.

# CONTENTS

The Chairman and his Wife

# Don't have it off with your secretary. Have it off with someone else's secretary.

The Managing Director and his Secretary

# The greatest labour-saving of today is... TOMORROW

The Senior Executive

# I used to be indecisive, but now I'm not too sure.

The Junior Executive

# I don't meet competition—I crush it!

The Sales Representative

# Some are bent with toil and some get crooked trying to avoid it.

The Shop Steward

# A girl's best friends are her legs — but even best friends must sometimes be parted.

MISS KILROY WAS HERE

The Office Romeo

The Office Cleaner

# TO THE TRAINS

who appear by courtesy of ASLEF

The train arriving at platforms 1, 2, 3, 4, and 5 is coming in sideways

It's quicker by ~~rail~~ SNAIL

DO YOUR BIT FOR UNEMPLOYMENT—GIVE SOMEONE YOUR JOB!

NO SCOTS PLEASE

OUT OF ORDER PLEASE USE PLATFORMS 3-4 & 7-8

# HOW TO BE A HAPPY COMMUTER

The contented commuter always has a song in his heart on his way to work – this song:

THE COMMUTER'S BARGING SONG

Jolly commuting weather
With snow up to your knees,
Trudging to the station,
There to sit and freeze.
Huddled up in the waiting-room,
With your bodies between your knees.
Huddled up in the waiting-room,
With your bodies between your knees.

The Krauts may be more brainy,
The Wops may make more row,
But we struggle on together,
Stolid, resigned and cowed,
For nothing in life can ever
Be worse than the eight-ten from Slough.
For nothing in life can ever
Be worse than the eight-ten from Slough.

Others may take your places
Standing in the queue,
While we pant down the platform
Barging to get through.
And puce will be our faces
As we squeeze inside the tube,
And puce will be our faces
As we squeeze inside the tube.

If you aren't fired with enthusiasm, you'll <u>be</u> fired with enthusiasm!

WE'RE FAR TOO BUSY TO WORK HERE!

A COMMITTEE IS A GROUP WHICH KEEPS MINUTES AND WASTES HOURS.

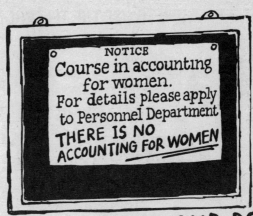

NOTICE

Course in accounting
for women.
For details please apply
to Personnel Department
THERE IS NO
ACCOUNTING FOR WOMEN

WHEN ALL IS SAID AND DONE,
THERE'S MORE THAT'S SAID
THAN DONE!

I wish I were what I was when
I wished I were what I am.

# HOW TO USE THE TELEPHONE

Apart from the kettle, the telephone is probably the most important piece of machinery in your office. As a link with the outside world, as a source of ever-growing information and as a means of keeping in touch with your friends for nothing, the office telephone is essential to business life.

There are two golden rules that will enable you to get the maximum benefit from your telephone;

(1) It is quite unnecessary to prolong any conversation over humdrum matters like contracts, delivery dates, complaints and orders. With only limited time at your disposal, the weather, the latest television programmes, the state of the family, must all take priority. In this day and age it's people that count, after all.

(2) As a public relations tool the telephone is second to none. More dates have been clinched over the phone than were ever made in a dance-hall. The tone of your voice, the excuse you make up for the liaison, the place from where you are phoning can all be conveniently disguised by the correct use of the telephone.

As long as *you* are making the phone call, there should never be any trouble. Problems begin when people start telephoning you. Experience has taught that it is not possible to drink a cup of tea, or eat an office biscuit while conducting a telephone conversation. Under these circumstances you must get the caller to ring back.

As far as telephone language is concerned there are certain expressions that will be found of great value when answers and replies have to be given which may not be to the caller's liking. A list of the most common of these is given as guidance:

| THE TRUTH | WHAT YOU SHOULD SAY |
|---|---|
| I don't want to take the call. | Hello ... hello ... hello (repeated after the caller has started speaking). |
| No. | O.K.; all right. |
| No. | I'd like to think about it. |
| Prelude to cutting off. | Will you hold the line please? |
| About to be dropped in the bin. | I'll give Mr ... your message. |
| He doesn't want to speak to you. | I'm sorry there's no reply. |
| He won't be in till 4.00. | I'm afraid Mr ... has just popped out for lunch |
| Perhaps you'll get the message. | I've tried to ring you several times. |
| Wednesday's golf day. | Mr ... has been called away to Head Office today. |
| He's knocking off his secretary. | Mr ... is busy dictating at the moment. |
| He's knocking off the other secretary. | Certainly, I'll connect you right away, Mrs ... |

**NOTICE**
Miss Baxter has been appointed to act as general supervisor of Work Area Six and not (as stated previously) of Work Area Sex.

**NOTICE**
Members of staff (embracing ladies) are requested not to loiter in the corridors.

**THOUGHT FOR TODAY**
A career woman is one who prefers to go out and take orders rather than stay at home and be the boss.

WOMEN ARE THE BEST OTHER SEX MEN HAVE

A SECRETARY IS A GIRL YOU PAY TO LEARN TO TYPE WHILE SHE'S LOOKING FOR A HUSBAND.

**A sexist is a man who scrawls balls on walls.**

# HOW TO USE THE DICTATING MACHINE

1. The start of the letter will be indicated by the words: 'Oh hell, the ****ing battery's run down again.'

2. Paragraphs will be indicated by a sneeze.

3. Full stops, question marks, colons, semi-colons, dashes and exclamation marks can be ignored unless an audible yawn is heard.

4. Commas will occur at the end of each breath. The dictator need only dictate for the duration of each breath. Where he or she pauses, a comma should be entered.

5. Parenthesis will be indicated by the inclusion of any word which is unprintable either here, or in any letter.

6. The apostrophe will be indicated by a raising of the voice; the thumping of the desk; the sound of smashing in the background.

7. Instructions for headings will precede the words of the heading, e.g. 'Let's try and get it right this time shall we, cloth-ears? – Monthly Sales Prospective Number 8.'

8. The twenty-four hour clock shall be dictated as spoken, e.g. 16.45, or when Noddy is pointing at 9 and Biggy Ears is pointing at 4.

9. Abbreviations will be dictated to show whether stops are required or not, e.g. 'Norwich – capitals: N stop O stop R stop W stop I stop C stop H stop – Nickers Off Ready When I Come Home – Yes, Miss.... "Nickers" should be spelt with a K but I'm employing poetic licence – amongst other things.'

Of course, if your company doesn't run to dictating machines, you'll simply have to dictate to your secretary in person ...

'O.K. – got another pencil? Last one ...
Dear Sir,
Right. What can I tell the boring old fart. Begin – In answer to your enquiry of the eighth last I am surprised to learn that you have been experiencing difficulties with your recent purchase. As you know the lorry you bought from us had always given perfect satisfaction until its sale. We had to flog it quick before the engine dropped out and the rear diff went for a burton; the silly bugger coughed up nine hundred quid for it. New paragraph.

As you know, we take care in inspecting all of our used vehicles thoroughly before parting with them. Your lorry was in first-class condition when it left our workshops. That's a stunning outfit you've got on. New, isn't it? New paragraph.

Might I respectfully suggest that your driver might be at fault? Four miles to the gallon certainly is very poor mileage for a vehicle such as yours. Four gallons to the mile is what we were getting from it down hill at the end. You know I'd never noticed that dimple there, but then we don't get many secretaries like you in this firm. However, as we always endeavour to provide a comprehensive back-up service to all of our customers, perhaps you would care to bring the vehicle round to us so that one of our expert mechanics can make any necessary adjustments to the engine. That should shut him up. Post it second class.

Yours sincerely,
Just sign it yourself. Well, what about that lunch ...'

OUT TO LUNCH
-IF NOT BACK
BY FIVE OUT
TO DINNER ALSO

Owing to the fuel
crisis, officials
are advised to take
advantage of their
secretaries between
12 p.m. and 2 p.m.

SHE WAS ONLY
THE MORSE
CODE OPERATOR'S
DAUGHTER, BUT
SHE DID IT DID IT
DID DID DID IT

WARNING – NIGHT WATCHMAN
PATROLS THIS AREA 24 HOURS A DAY.

Any person passing this
point will be drowned by
order of the management.

THE SPARE KEY TO THE FIRST
AID ROOM IS AVAILABLE IN
THE FIRST AID ROOM.

# HOW TO HANDLE YOUR CORRESPONDENCE

The best business letters are true works of literature. Here are some genuine examples to help inspire you ...

Dear Sir,

    With reference to our letter re Majorca tour, the flight you mention is completely booked, but we will inform you immediately someone falls out, as usually happens.

Dear Madam,

    With reference to your blue raincoat, our manufacturers have given the garment in question a thorough testing, and find that it is absolutely waterproof. If you will wear it on a dry day, and then take it off and examine it, you will see that our statement is correct.

Dear Madam,

    In reply to your letter, we are very sorry for the delay in sending the house-coat, but the tremendous demand for these has denuded our stock. We are, however, expecting further delay in a day or so.

Sir,

For the case that your electric light should fail we beg to send you enclosed a postcard which please send us at once when you find your light out. The company will then send you another postcard.

Yours truly,

Manager, Siam Electricity Co. Ltd.

Dear Sir stroke Madam,

Would you please try your telephone now, and if you are unable to use it would you please report the difficulty by dialling 151.

Dear Member,

This rule is included as a concession solely to cover the position of members who died whilst they were away on sick leave at reduced rates. It was contemplated that they would pay up any arrears on return to duty.

Dear Colleagues,

Since the former secretary had left the area and the former minutes could not be found, it was moved, seconded and carried that the minutes of the last meeting be adopted, as they would have been read had they been found.

Dear Customer,

The British firm Digitronics Ltd. has changed its name to Digitronix Ltd, to avoid confusion with a US firm with a similar sounding name.

Dear Sir/Madam,

You have been served with your cactus by our Rainwear Staff. We have unfortunately been unable to teach our computer the difference between an umbrella and a cactus. Therefore, on your next monthly statement, your cactus will be described as an umbrella.

Dear Subscriber,

If you bought our course: *How to fly in six easy lessons*, we apologize for any inconvenience caused by our failure to include the last chapter, titled: *How to land your plane safely*. Send us your name and address and we will forward it to you post haste.

Dear Sir,

The title of the film *Plink Plonk Plink* (F52377), registered on 7 June, 1967, has been corrected to read *Plink Plunk Plink*.

Sir,

It is regretted that it was not possible to send the enclosed forms to you before the date by which, had you received them, you would be required to forward completed copies to this office.

BE WARNED: If you don't send out the right kind of letter, you won't get the right kind of reply ... This letter was sent by an Australian stamp collector to his supplier:

Sir,

I am intensely dissatisfied with your organization and shall recommend it to the Russians as a prime nuclear target.

You are confused as to what the problem is. Let me explain while I have some workable sanity left:
(1) I receive a set of covers in due order.
(2) I send off my payment in due order.
(3) 60 to 90 days later I get a past due notice.
(4) I panic.
(5) I check my records and find that I have paid in due order and therefore your notice is all wrong.
(6) This has happened with every issue since May '77.
(7) I gnash my teeth, pull my hair and rend my garments.
(8) I complain but nobody listens.

Now I find that I have received and paid for 25 sets or $125 worth. Set #25 is not accounted for in your letter. I sent you payment for that one way back in ancient times, so you should have a record of it, but I just have the absolute feeling that I will soon be receiving a past due notice for it.

I have no choice therefore but to visit upon you my own particular divine wrath and *cancel my subscription.*

# IF TIME IS MONEY, WE'RE ALL LIVING BEYOND OUR MEANS

A workers rights are those which belong to him which he can't have.

The only person to get everything done by Friday was Robinson Crusoe!

# HOW TO MAKE YOUR EXCUSES

A.M.
'He hasn't come in yet.'
'I expect him in any minute.'
'He just sent word in he'd be a little late.'
'He's been in, but he went out again.'
'He's gone to lunch.'

P.M.
'I expect him in any minute.'
'He hasn't come back yet. Can I take a message?'
'He's somewhere in the building. His coat is here.'
'Yes, he was in, but he went out again.'
'I don't know whether he'll be back or not.'
'No, he's gone for the day.'

Don't vote Labour– vote TGWU
and cut out the middleman.

# WHEN IT COMES TO GIVING THIS FIRM STOPS AT NOTHING!

When you're right in this
office, no one remembers.
When you're wrong,
no one forgets!

People speak about
unemployment as if
work was a four-letter word.

WHY WASTE TIME WORKING EIGHT
HOURS A DAY JUST TO BECOME THE
BOSS AND WORK TWELVE HOURS A DAY.

He who hesitates is bossed!

# HOW TO COMMUNICATE BY NUMBERS

If you need an excuse, just think of a number ...

**AUTOMATIC EXCUSES**

1. I thought I told you.
2. That's the way we've always done it.
3. No one told me to go ahead.
4. I didn't think it was that important.
5. I'm so busy I just couldn't get around to it.
6. Why bother? The Boss won't buy it.
7. I didn't know you were in a hurry for it.
8. That's his job, not mine.
9. I forgot.
10. I'm waiting for the OK.
11. That's not my department.
12. How did I know this was different.
13. Wait until the Boss comes back and ask him.

In the interests of efficiency and harmonious industrial relations the management have installed a computer to deal with all internal dialogue. Employees are requested to express their views by number from now on.

1. It's a return to the 1920s.
2. We've been doing it this way for forty years.
3. This company is different.
4. Maybe, but we're not in Japan, are we.
5. Look what happened to Chrysler.
6. We've never done it before.
7. We don't have the facilities.
8. Not until our previous demands are met.
9. It won't work in a small company.
10. It won't work in a large company.
11. It won't work in this company.
12. Our brothers fought for forty years to stop it.
13. Why change when it's working OK?
14. Not now you've done away with our differentials.
15. What about our differentials?
16. What's the catch?
17. We don't have the manpower.
18. You can't teach an old dog new tricks.
19. The lads will never buy it.
20. Who do you think you are – Sir Michael Edwardes?
21. It's against union policy.
22. With three million unemployed you must be joking.
23. You may be able to con the other lads, but we'll be out.
24. Don't think you'd win if it went to arbitration.
25. With this equipment, you must be kidding.
26. This is the thin end of the wedge.
27. We're doing all right as it is.
28. The union's not ready for it.
29. It's too much trouble to change.

30. It needs sleeping on.
31. The night shift won't like it.
32. It's not our problem.
33. It's not my job.
34. It won't work in this section.
35. It's never been done in this firm.
36. They'd call us blacklegs.
37. You want all that and a productivity agreement, too?
38. If it works there, let them keep it.
39. It can't be done.
40. So what.
41. Not until we get the thirty-five hour week.
42. The canteen staff say it can't be done.
43. You'll have to agree with the other branches first.
44. It'll make a mockery of the negotiation procedure.
45. What's it worth?
46. This isn't Poland.
47. It'll have to go to the executive.
48. And who's to say you're right anyway?
49. Over my dead body.
50. **** ***!

# THE WORLD IS FULL OF SURPRISES – FEW OF THEM ARE PLEASANT – TRY WORKING HERE.

God might have created the world in six days, but he didnt have to do it in triplicate!!!

## Going to a psychiatrist didn't cure my drink problem –I kept falling off the couch.

MOST OF US WOULD ENJOY THE DAY MORE IF IT STARTED LATER!

## Doing a good job here is like wetting yourself in a dark suit; you get a warm feeling...

## ...but nobody notices.

# Credit must be given to the worker with a large family
## —he can't live without it!

# HOW TO SAVE ENERGY AND IMPROVE EFFICIENCY

ENERGY – EXPENDITURE AND ECONOMIES

In the light of government directives to save energy the Board has undertaken an exhaustive survey of the stress factors born by employees in the course of their work. The following statistics indicate the broad outlines of the findings.

The figures relate to the number of calories expended in any given activity in any given period of sixty minutes (1 hour):

| | |
|---|---|
| Running fast | 975 |
| Running moderately fast | 850 |
| Climbing stairs at 2.5 km/h | 620 |
| Walking at 6.5 km/h | 492 |
| Driving car | 168 |
| Standing | 118 |
| Sitting and writing | 114 |
| Sitting | 108 |
| Lying in bed | 60 |

As a result of this survey the Board has concluded that:

(a) All employees should endeavour to travel to work by car, ideally with someone else driving.
(b) They should avoid using the stairs whenever possible.
(c) The firm should move into brand-new single-storey offices.
(d) Offices will be equipped with beds to replace the stress-intensive furniture currently in use.
(e) The Sports Club be disbanded forthwith.
(f) All correspondence will be sent verbally with immediate effect.

It is hoped that all employees will do their utmost to follow these simple instructions as part of our efforts to respond to the government's initiative to curb energy waste.

To be inspired by a real efficiency expert in action, read his report on a concert given recently at London's Royal Festival Hall ...

During much of the work period, the four oboe players had nothing to do. Their numbers should be reduced and their work should be distributed more evenly throughout the work period, so eliminating peaks of activity.

The twelve violin players were all playing identical notes. This is unnecessary duplication. This section should be drastically pruned. If the resultant cuts lead to a reduction in sound, electronic apparatus will more than make up for the loss in manpower.

Considerable time was spent in the playing of demi-semi-quavers; this seems to be an unnecessary refinement. It is recommended, therefore, that all notes be rounded up to the nearest semi-quaver. If this practice was adopted, it would make it possible to employ trainees and lower-grade operatives more extensively.

Similarly there is excessive repetition of many musical passages. There is wide scope for modification and reduction here. Little contribution is made by repeating on the woodwind a passage that has already been dealt with thoroughly by the strings. If all such redundant passages were eliminated, it is estimated that the whole work period, currently two hours, could be reduced to twenty minutes, which would also obviate the need for an interval.

The conductor has been consulted about these recommendations and is generally in agreement with them, though the opinion was expressed that there might be some falling off in box-office receipts. If this indeed proves to be the case, it should be possible to close sections of the auditorium entirely. This would result in additional savings in overhead expenses, heating, lighting, attendance, etc. And if the worst came to the worst, the entire programme could be shut down and the public could attend a similar work period at the Albert Hall instead.

If you can't get your work done in twenty-four hours, work nights.

THIS WAY UP IF YOU WANT TO SEE A HEALTHY PROFIT.

Never fall into the trap of confusing motion with progress.

A 5-day week is just a 4-day week that takes a little longer to get through

And on the fifth day God saw that it was good...and rested.

The reason for the rush is the delay, and the reason for the delay is the rush!

IF IT LOOKS EASY, IT'S GOING TO BE HARD. IF IT LOOKS HARD, IT'S GOING TO BE DAMN'NEAR IMPOSSIBLE

Bees are never as busy as they sound – they just don't know how to buzz slower.

ZZZZZZ

ZZZZ

The first 90% of the task takes 10% of the time and the last 10% takes 90% of the time.

# HOW TO LIVE WITH A COMPUTER

Learn the rules of the game ...

(1) Any given programme, when running, is obsolete.
(2) Any given programme costs more and takes longer.
(3) If a programme is useful, it will have to be changed.
(4) Any given programme will expand to fill all available memory.
(5) If a programme is useless, it will be documented.
(6) The value of a programme is proportional to the volume of its output.
(7) Programme complexity grows until it exceeds the capability of the programmer who must maintain it.
(8) Make it possible for programmers to write programmes in English, and you will find that programmers cannot write English.

(1) The world's best programmer has to be someone.
(2) The more humanlike a computer becomes, the less it spends time computing and the more it spends time doing more humanlike work.
(3) A software committee of one is limited by its own horizon and will specify software only that far.
(4) When the system programmers declare the system works, it has worked and will work again some day.

THIS COMPUTER (XB20) HAS BEEN PROGRAMMED TO EXTERMINATE ANYONE WHO TRIES TO ATTEMPT TO PROGRAMME SAME FOR SPACE INVADERS.

DON'T WORRY ABOUT COMPUTERS.
IF THEY GET TOO POWERFUL, JUST
ORGANISE THEM INTO COMMITTEES.

Computerised gossip
    is just micro-chip-chat.

IF GOD HAD MEANT US TO GO
METRIC, WHY DID HE GIVE
JESUS TWELVE DISCIPLES?

The cause of problems
            are solutions!

Efficiency is just a highly developed form of laziness.

ALL THE WORLD'S AN ANALOG STAGE, AND DIGITAL CIRCUITS PLAY ONLY BIT PARTS.

The length of any meeting rises with the square of the number of people present.

USE YOUR HEAD – IT'S THE LITTLE THINGS THAT COUNT!

# HOW TO RUN THE PERSONNEL DEPARTMENT

To run a personnel department successfully you have got
to be able to recognise the true qualities and potential of
prospective employees ...

| | | POTENTIAL | |
| --- | --- | --- | --- |
| | | OUTSTANDING | HIGHLY SATISFACTORY |
| | OVERALL ABILITY | Leaps tall buildings with a single bound | Needs running start to jump tall buildings |
| | TIMELINESS | Faster than speeding bullet | Only as fast as speeding bullet |
| QUALITIES | INITIATIVE | Stronger than locomotive | Stronger than bull elephant |
| | ADAPTABILITY | Walks on water consistently | Only walks on water in emergencies |
| | COMMUNICATION | Talks with God | Talks with angels |
| | RELATIONSHIP | Belongs in general management | Belongs in executive ranks |
| | PLANNING | Too bright to worry | Worries about future |

| SATISFACTORY | LESS SATISFACTORY | UNSATISFACTORY |
| --- | --- | --- |
| Can only leap small buildings | Crashes into buildings | Cannot recognize buildings |
| Somewhat slower than bullet | Can only shoot bullets | Wounds self with bullets |
| Stronger than bull | Shoots bull | Smells like bull |
| Washes with water | Drinks water | Passes water in emergencies |
| Talks to self | Argues with self | Loses those arguments |
| Belongs in rank and file | Belongs behind broom | Belongs with competitor |
| Worries about present | Worries about past | Too thick to worry |

You also need to master the precise language of the seasoned personnel officer ...

In line with the new plans for reorganizing the Personnel Department the following phrases are to be employed when completing staff reports. These reports are to remain 'open'. However, in the interests of efficiency the following meanings will be attached to each one:

| | |
|---|---|
| Keen sense of humour | Tells endless strings of dirty jokes – idle. |
| Zealous attitude | Opinionated. |
| Unlimited potential | Will stay with us until retirement. |
| Tactful in dealings with superiors | Knows when to keep his/her mouth shut. |
| Maintains professional attitude | A snob. |
| Conscientious and careful | Easily intimidated. |
| Stern disciplinarian | A right sod. |
| Slightly below average | Thick as two short planks. |
| Forceful and aggressive | Argumentative. |
| Character above reproach | We haven't caught up with him/her yet. |
| Indifferent to instruction | Knows more than we do. |
| Active socially | Drinks heavily. |
| Average | Not too bright. |
| Gets along extremely well with subordinates and superiors alike | Chicken. |
| Willing to spend extra hours in the office | Wretched home life. |
| Strong adherence to principles | Pig-headed. |
| Quick thinking | Never short of a plausible excuse for errors. |

| | |
|---|---|
| Expresses himself/herself well | Speaks English. |
| Approaches difficult problems logically | Gets someone else to carry the can. |
| A keen analyst | Thoroughly confused. |
| Of great value to the company | Turns in work on time. |
| Never misses any advantage to progress | Buys drinks for superiors. |
| Meticulous attention to detail | Can't see the wood for the trees. |
| Judgement is usually sound | Lucky. |
| Not a 'desk' man | No higher education. |
| Demonstrates qualities of leadership | Loud mouth. |

When assessing staff for possible promotion you may find it helpful to use this form ...

---

**STAFF ASSESSMENT**

Employee's Name      Department

Assessed by      Date

---

Put cross through appropriate rating in each case:

MIEN      Low    High

(a) Gestures:—V-signs and their frequency;    1 2 3 4 5 6
variety of faces pulled

(b) Dress:—yes or no; Hepworths, Marks    1 2 3 4 5 6
and Sparks; Jaeger; or Austin Reed

(c) Courtesy:—buys drinks for boss;    1 2 3 4 5 6
compliments boss's wife; drives older
car than boss

(d) Fitness:—can handle 18 holes before    1 2 3 4 5 6
drinks at 11.00 am; can't do above;
uses lift; travels by Southern Region

(e) Poise:—ability to hold drink; threw up    1 2 3 4 5 6
at office party.


SOCIAL INTERACTION

(a) Participation in social activities:—who's    1 2 3 4 5 6
he knocking off in the typing pool; are
you jealous; does he stand a cat in
hell's chance with the boss's daughter?

(b) Participation in local affairs:—does he/    1 2 3 4 5 6
she have a criminal record; does this
have any bearing on his/her work?
wife-swapping; gossip-monger

(c) Ability to mix with people:—    1 2 3 4 5 6
smooth-talking; socially inadequate;
always plastered

(d) Attitudes with other people:—fascist;    1 2 3 4 5 6
'liberal'; agrees with management;
enjoys canteen food; (if male) does *not*
lust after managing director's secretary.

## PSYCHOLOGICAL EQUILIBRIUM SITUATION

(a) Reaction to stress:—total panic; the bottle; iron resolve; Valium   1 2 3 4 5 6

(b) General competence:—supreme; average; hopeless   1 2 3 4 5 6

(c) Degree of personal motivation at work:—(more degrees, less motivation)   1 2 3 4 5 6

(d) Childhood, adolescence and family background:—deprived; depraved; bourgeois; delinquent; Oedipus complex; chorister; brownie; listened to Uncle Mac; believed in Father Christmas; still believes in Father Christmas   1 2 3 4 5 6

## LEADERSHIP

(a) Experience of leadership:—if employee works immediately beneath you, how good are you; how often have you been absent leaving employee to hold the baby; how disastrous was this; if not disastrous, how come you're still with us?   1 2 3 4 5 6

(b) Leadership motivation:—power-crazy; needs money to support mistress; will soon need money to pay alimony; wants a worker's state; wants change of office/car; needs promotion to get out of your hair; has nice legs which are wasted in .......... at present.   1 2 3 4 5 6

## MATURITY

(a) Senile; middle-aged (10 years older than you); precocious; one foot in the grave; one foot in the pram   1 2 3 4 5 6

(b) Personal drive:—best average distance over par four hole; wind direction; type of club used. (Nothing lower than '3' need be entered)   1 2 3 4 5 6

(c) Responsibility:—easy to blame; can be pinned down; slimy operator; obvious scapegoat; number of cock-ups in last twelve months   1 2 3 4 5 6

As every good personnel officer knows, when it comes to recruiting it pays to advertise ...

# WANTED –
# A FIRST CLASS MALE WAITRESS
## ONLY QUALIFIED PERSONS CONSIDERED

**WANTED** – Part-time hotel receptionist and telephone operator (small broad). Apply Hotel Nicosia.

Cordon Bleu cook required for government department dining room. Good salary, excellent working conditions, bonuses, plus luncheon vouchers.

Unusual opportunity for biscuit salesman with a modern institution; Must have at least 2 years experience within last 6 months or do not apply.

Gentlemen required, knowledge of shorthand absolutely essential though not necessary.

## TWO BUSINESS LADIES REQUIRE SLEEPING PARTNER FOR BEAUTY SALON

**WANTED –** Some additional female technicians at the fast-expanding Charles River Breeding Laboratory

Woman wanted to run up curtains.

Receptionist - telephonist required. - Must be prepared to work very occasional Saturday mornings (often).

**WANTED –** Cigarette makers (female) round and flat.

Revlon Ltd. require a SENIOR BEAUTY ADVISOR for a York store. Applicants should be mature cowmen.

I'd advise you to follow the Lone Ranger's example, ma'am, and wear a mask.

ADVISOR

Tea Room Attendant required. Knowledge of first aid essential.

Lady required for six hours work per week to clean small officers at Station Road, Witney.

**LADIES!** We are looking for caféteria insistants to work in our modern caféteria in the Grove Road Area. Successful applicants will be asked to work occasially.

Gravedigger's assistant wanted. Must be dead keen.

Woman required for looking over fixed bats and cranks in warehouse.

The organisation of this place is like a septic tank —
Only the really big lumps rise to the top!

ONLY THE MEDIOCRE WORKER IS ALWAYS AT HIS BEST.

Hell knows no fury like a planner scorned.

Make sure brain is engaged before putting mouth in gear.

# HOW TO BE A TROUBLE SHOOTER

If you want to be a successful trouble-shooter, these are the rules. Read on ...

(a) Profess not to have *the* answer. This lets you out of having *any* answer.

(b) Say that we must not move too rapidly. This avoids the need of getting started.

(c) For every proposal set up an opposite and conclude that the 'middle ground' (no motion whatever) represents the wisest course of action.

(d) Point out that any attempt to reach a conclusion is only a futile 'quest for certainty'. Doubt and uncertainty promote growth.

(e) When in a tight place say something that the group cannot understand.

(f) Argue that the problem 'cannot be separated' from other problems; therefore no problem can be solved until all other problems are solved.

(g) Point out that those who see the problem do so by virtue of personality traits, e.g. they are unhappy and transfer their dissatisfaction to the area under discussion.

(h) Ask what is meant by the question. When it is clarified there will be no time left for the answer.

(i) Retreat from the problem into endless discussion of various techniques for approaching it.

(j) Retreat into analogies and discuss them until everyone has forgotten the original problem.

(k) Point out that some of the greatest minds have struggled with the problem, implying that it does us credit to have thought of it.

(l) Be thankful for the problem. It has stimulated our best thinking and has, therefore, contributed to our growth. It (the problem) should get a medal.

Nothing vouchered, nothing gained.

BE POLITE TO EVERYBODY UNTIL YOU MAKE YOUR FIRST MILLION —AFTER THAT, EVERYBODY WILL BE POLITE TO *YOU*!

MONEY IS THE ROOT OF ALL EVIL...AND A MAN NEEDS ROOTS

The man who can smile when things go wrong has thought of the person he can blame it on.

71

# HOW TO MASTER THE LANGUAGE OF BUSINESS

The successful operator in the modern world of business
needs to have a feeling for poetry ...


I had a little document,
As pure as driven snow,
Yet everywhere that paper went,
It wandered to and fro.

I thought that people gladly
And swiftly would concur,
But while I waited sadly,
They'd cavil and demur.

Some thought the paper much too short;
Others much too long.
Some thought the language much too weak;
Others much too strong.

So by the time that document came dawdling back my way
It made no difference where it went –
The issue was passé!

## THE EXECUTIVE LOQUACULATOR

If you have no natural flair for language don't despair, the Executive Loquaculator is here ...

It has come to our attention that certain senior personnel have been singularly lacking in the modern-as-tomorrow, authoritative, contract-winning terminology that this company needs to maintain its place in our market sector. Accordingly the Board has undertaken an in-depth survey to provide all management and senior grades with an easy-to-use, fact-fudging instrument which will provide three words, where, until now, a pause has had to suffice.

By selecting any word from each of the three columns it is hoped that the users will be able to sharpen up their language while successfully glossing over any embarrassing details that they may be forced to expose from time to time.

The choice is almost endless – USE IT.

| | | | |
|---|---|---|---|
| 1 | Permanent | Concordant | Interdependence |
| 2 | Positivistic | Digital | Structure |
| 3 | Bilateral | Imitative | Polarity |
| 4 | Partial | Discrepant | Specification |
| 5 | Flanking | Recessive | Implication |
| 6 | Divergent | Expansive | Affinity |
| 7 | Quantitative | Decentralized | Potency |
| 8 | Integrated | Contributory | Motivation |
| 9 | Gradual | Incremental | Flexibility |
| 10 | Ultimative | Monitored | Factionalism |
| 11 | Intransigent | Innovative | Diffusion |
| 12 | Responsive | Convergent | Escalation |
| 13 | Differentiated | Dynamic | Feasibility |
| 14 | Nonfragmenting | Logistical | Periodicity |
| 15 | Predicative | Conglomerate | Consistency |
| 16 | Temporal | Differential | Accumulation |
| 17 | Synchronized | Aggregating | Transcendence |
| 18 | Structural | Eliminative | Solidification |
| 19 | Representative | Diversifying | Competence |
| 20 | Societal | Homogeneous | Adaptation |
| 21 | Obsolete | Universal | Capability |
| 22 | Systematized | Fluctuating | Projection |
| 23 | Parallel | Simulated | Extension |
| 24 | Dialectical | Identifying | Mobility |
| 25 | Compatible | Usurpative | Expectancy |
| 26 | Gradual | Transitional | Phase |
| 27 | Multilateral | Culminating | Concept |
| 28 | Optional | Complementary | Classification |
| 29 | Indicative | Deteriorative | Plasticity |
| 30 | Functional | Elongating | Mobility |
| 31 | Reversibile | Prior | Eventuality |
| 32 | Determinative | Exponential | Extrapolation |
| 33 | Global | Allocated | Transparency |
| 34 | Total | Participatory | Efficiency |
| 35 | Substantial | Restrictive | Time phase |
| 36 | Balanced | Transfigurative | Options |
| 37 | Concentrated | Programmed | Equivalence |
| 38 | Synchronous | Reciprocal | Projection |
| 39 | contradictory | Organizational | Vacancy |
| 40 | Interfractional | Uniform | Programming |
| 41 | Distributive | Progressive | Permanence |
| 42 | Inductive | Unilateral | Synthesis |
| 43 | Coherent | Management | Application |
| 44 | Proliferative | Co-operative | Sufficiency |
| 45 | Compatible | Coincidental | Finality |
| 46 | Ameliorating | Exemplificatory | Discontinuity |
| 47 | Descriptive | Erupting | Cancellation |
| 48 | Ambivalent | Component | Denudation |
| 49 | Existential | Obstructive | Epigenesis |
| 50 | Coincidental | Illusory | Disparity |

## EXECUTIVE VOCABULARY

Understanding what's *really* being said.

| | |
|---|---|
| Automatic | Can't repair it yourself. |
| Bank | Institution which will lend you an umbrella and demand its return as soon as it rains. |
| Blackleg | Eccentric who treats the right to work as if it was for real. |
| Boss | Relatively low-cost, automatic device installed by senior management to spy on work force. |
| Career defence | Cover your backside. |
| Cash | The working man's credit card. |
| Coffee break | Opportunity to buy cup of coffee for under 20p. |
| Conference | Place where conversation is substituted for the dreariness of labour and the loneliness of thought. <br> – A meeting of the bored. |
| Consultant | Person who borrows your watch to tell you the time before walking off with the watch. <br> – Unemployed practitioner. |
| Coordinator | The person who has a desk between two expediters. |
| Discussion | General pooling of ignorance. |
| Expedite | To confound confusion with commotion. |
| Good idea | One your boss is convinced he/she thought of first. |
| Industrial tribunal | Welfare agency from which workers may collect bonuses for being sacked. |

| | |
|---|---|
| In conference | Never available when you want him/her. |
| In due course | Never. |
| Keen worker | One that looks for something to occupy his/her time after he/she has been given a job. |
| Living wage | Sum covering broad financial spectrum governed by whether you're giving or receiving. |
| Memorandum | Something written, not to inform the reader but to protect the writer. |
| Moderate | One who makes enemies left and right. |
| Nationalized industry | One that expands by contracting debt. |
| Occupational hazard | Having to work occasionally. |
| Policy | Convenient shield offering shelter in case of disaster or enquiry. |
| Programme | Any assignment that cannot be dealt with by one phone call. |
| Recession | When your neighbour loses his job (not to be confused with 'depression' – when you lose yours) |
| Rich man | Poor man with money. |
| Slogan | Ancient substitute for argument or fact. |

*Sources*

| | |
|---|---|
| Reliable source | The person you just met. |
| Informed source | The person who told the person you just met. |
| Unimpeachable source | The person who started the rumour in the first place. |
| The very best authority | Your own guesswork. |
| Steady worker | One up from motionless worker. |
| Taxpayer | Person who doesn't need to take a Civil Service exam to work for the Government. |
| Top priority | It's idiotic, but the boss wants it. |

| | |
|---|---|
| Correct within an order of magnitude | Wrong |
| It is clear that much additional work will be required before a complete understanding ... | I haven't a clue |
| Let's take a survey | We need more time to think of an answer |
| It might be argued that ... | I have such a good answer to this objection that I shall now raise it |
| The most reliable values are those of Jones | He trained under me |
| These results will be reported at a later date | I might possibly get round to it sometime |
| For your consideration | You hold the bag for a while |
| Three of these samples were chosen for detailed study | The results on the others didn't make sense and were ignored |
| ... accidentally stained during mounting | ... dropped on the floor |
| ... handled with extreme care throughout the experiments | ... nearly dropped on the floor |
| Competition elimination | Screw your buddies |
| Developed after years of intensive research | Discovered by accident |
| Typical results are shown | The best results are shown |
| Give us the benefit of your wide experience in this field | We don't mind listening to you since we've already decided what course to follow |

| | |
|---|---|
| It is hoped that this work will stimulate further investigation in this field | This report isn't up to much, but neither is any of the other work on this miserable subject |
| Let's get together on this | I reckon you're as confused as I am |
| Take under advisement | Ignore and hope everyone will forget it |
| Approved, subject to comment | Redraft the damned thing |
| Although some detail has been lost in reproduction, it is clear from the original micrograph | It is impossible to tell a thing from the micrograph |
| Give someone the picture, to | To make a long, confused and inaccurate statement to a newcomer |
| Verbal containment | Shut your mouth |
| Under active consideration | We're searching the files for it |
| Under consideration | Never heard of it |
| The agreement with the predicted curve is excellent | Fair |
| ... good | Poor |
| ... satisfactory | Doubtful |
| ... fair | Imaginary |
| ... is in the process | ... is so wrapped up in red tape that any progress is hopeless |
| We will advise you in due course | If we can work it out, we'll be in touch |

For examples of the language of business at its most eloquent, poetic and powerful, read on. Every quotation is guaranteed genuine ...

*From a patent application:*
Apparatus from removing casings from sausages and the like (US Patent No. 2,672,646)

In a sausage-skinning machine, means for rotating a sausage about its longitudinal axis, means for simultaneously holding a part of the skin against rotative movement with the sausage to cause said skin to be torn off said sausage circumferentially, and means for simultaneously moving said sausage endwise with respect to said holding means, said rotating, holding and moving means being operatively related to one another to cause said skin to be torn off and stripped from the sausage helically.

*From the US Revenue Act 1940:*
Component corporations of component corporations – If a corporation is a component corporation of an acquiring corporation, under subsection (b) or under this subsection, it shall (except for the purpose of section 742d and section 743a) also be a component corporation of the corporation of which such acquiring corporation is a component corporation.

*From the house magazine of an American research laboratory:*
'Any employee whose current salary rate exceeds the new top of the salary range for his or her classification will not be eligible for the general increase unless the new top of the salary range for his or her classification exceeds the employee's current salary rate.'

*From the National Insurance Act 1959:*
'For the purpose of this Part of the Schedule a person over pensionable age, not being an insured person, shall be treated as an insured person if he would be an insured person were he under pensionable age and would be an employed person were he an insured person.'

*From the minutes of evidence taken by a Royal Commission on the Civil Service:*
'What I have said has demonstrated that it is very difficult to find an answer to that question, but if I were pressed for an answer I would say that, so far as we can see, taking it rather by and large, taking one time with another, and taking the average of Departments, it is probable that there would not be found to be very much in it either way.'

*From the Occupational Safety and Health Administration Rulebook – defining an exit as:*
'... that portion of a means of egress which is separated from all other spaces of the building or structure by construction or equipment as required in this subpart to provide a protected way of travel to the exit discharge.'

*and subsequently defining a 'means of egress' as:*
'... a continuous and unobstructed way of exit travel from any point in a building or structure to a public way and consists of three separate and distinct parts: the way of exit access, the exit and the way of exit discharge.'

*From an Australian circular on employment:*
The admission of domestic workers from abroad was confined to female applicants. This restriction has been relaxed. The term 'girl' now stands for any type of applicant regardless of sex.

*From a form issued to employers by the Department of Employment:*
'Separate departments of the same premises are treated as separate premises for this purpose where separate branches of work which are commonly carried on in separate premises are carried on in separate departments on the same premises.'

*From a letter sent out by the Department of Employment:*
'Unemployment benefit is not payable in respect of the dates quoted which cannot be treated as days of unemployment on the ground that the claimant notwithstanding that this employment has terminated received, by way of compensation for the loss of the remuneration which he would have received for that day each of those days if the unemployment had not been terminated, payment of an amount which exceeds the amount arrived at by deducting the standard daily rate of unemployment benefit from two-thirds of the remuneration lost in respect of that day each of those days.'

*From a Treasury circular:*
In conformity with a Treasury order which has just been issued, official correspondence should not refer to the 'devaluation of the £'. Some such phrase as 'the change in the dollar rate' should be used instead.

*From a report of Water Softening Sub-Committee of the Central Advisory Committee:*
'We do suggest, within very wide limits, washing a desirable habit.'

*From a Department of Trade bulletin:*
Leave Regulations – Section 3. When an employee absent
from duty on account of illness dies without making
application for advanced sick leave, the fact of death is
sufficient to show a 'serious disability' and to dispense with
the requirement of a formal application and a medical
certificate.

*From a BBC memorandum:*
Distinguish between an Extra and a Walk-on:
(1) A 'policeman' standing at the corner of a street, alone,
but not doing anything in particular, would be an
Extra. If he was called upon to do anything specific to
the action of a drama he becomes a Walk-on I; if he
speaks he is a Walk-on II.
(2) A 'barman' seen in long-shot busying himself in
normal barman work would be an extra; if he serves a
pint to a leading character on cue he becomes a Walk-
on I; if he speaks a few unimportant words, he
becomes a Walk-on II.
(3) A 'gardener' alone in a long-shot sweeping a drive
would be an Extra; if he is seen in close-up grimacing,
he becomes a Walk-on II.

From the pen of one of the true Bards of Bureaucracy:

THE INGRATITUDES

Cursed are the poor in spirit: for they never get a rise.
Cursed are they that moan: for they shall never be comforted.
Cursed are the meek: for they shall accept the management's offer.
Cursed are they which do hunger and thirst after canteen lunches: for all their complaints are just filed.
Cursed are the careful: for all they get are cares.
Cursed are the pure in heart: for they shall see through the rest of us.
Cursed are the peace-makers: for they shall be called scabs.
Cursed are they who are persecuted for righteousness' sake: for theirs is the dole queue.
Cursed are ye, when men shall revile you, and persecute you, and shall say all manner of evil against you falsely for the strike's sake.
Mourn, and be exceeding sad: for meagre is your reward in compensation: for so persecuted they the shop stewards who worked for you.

It was felt by the Luncheon Club Committee that although Crême Caramel was on the menu more frequently after the previous meeting, it had tended to drop off recently.

SAVE THE WHALE
–DON'T EAT HERE!

OFFICE USE ONLY

May also be used for coats.

Staff should empty the tea-pots and then stand upside down on tea trays.

# HOW TO MASTER DESK ARCHERY

For those moments of inactivity or intense frustration
when hands stray idly through desk drawers and usually
come to rest on rubber bands, paper clips, bottles of ink,
empty gin bottles, which alone serve no useful purpose,
DESK ARCHERY offers an entertaining, skilful and
demanding activity that will take you out of yourself and
prevent you from pushing your boss down the lift-shaft
or falling asleep over your desk out of sheer boredom.

For DESK ARCHERY all you will need are two raised fingers, or possibly one raised finger and one raised thumb, and three rubber bands.

The rubber bands are looped together to produce one long rubber band, which is then attached to the two raised digits to form a sling.

Projectiles may take many forms – lumps of Blu-tac; staples; pencils; folded strips of paper; or lumps of sugar. The only deciding factor in choosing your weapon is that it should make a mark on the target. (Strips of paper dipped in ink are usually the most popular – though you need to develop a good aim before getting too carried away.)

The game can be played individually to better a personal score, or between two or more players to decide who buys the first round/first asks for a rise/makes the next pot of tea.

In the absence of a suitable target, other than office personnel, this page has proved very successful in the limited space available to most competitors.

# FOOLS RUSH IN WHERE FOOLS HAVE BEEN BEFORE!

Experience is what you get when you failed to get what you wanted.

My boss is Irish. He's made me an offer I can't understand.

# Oil is thicker than blood!

AN OPTIMIST IS SOMEONE WHO'S NEVER HAD MUCH EXPERIENCE.

The man who knows 'how' will never be without a job. The man who knows 'why' will always be his boss.

# HOW TO SUCCEED IN BUSINESS WITHOUT DOING A THING

You too can create a professional paradise, your own Garden of Eden at the office, your own Heaven on the shop-floor. If only you know how to set about it, a workers' wonderland is yours ...

OFFICE YOU-TOPIA

In spite of what people say to the contrary there's only one person that matters in your office – you. If you want to cock things up, there's very little anyone else can do about it, and if they try, there's the Industrial Tribunal to see you right. However, careful planning and the creation of the right impression can provide a convincing camouflage at work that will let you get on with life, without being overburdened by other distractions between nine and five. It's all a matter of strategy.

## Work Planning

This always looks good. It doesn't require much effort and it certainly won't require any real work. Keenies plan their work by the day, the week and the month, so do the same. Simply list all the outstanding things you failed to do last week, last month and yesterday and put them down in one of those flashy desk diaries that multinationals give away at Christmas. Leave this lying around open at the relevant day and you shouldn't be too bothered with people finding things for you to do. Remember that even the best plans can be upset by emergencies. Flexibility is the name of the game and you should allow gaps in each schedule to accommodate: rail strikes; lengthy negotiations with the pretty clerk in charge of the stationery cupboard; tea-break consultations; visits to the bookies to see what odds they're offering on Kerry Packer buying British Leyland in order to get his hands on Lord's. Don't forget to cross off items as time passes – they can always be entered again later under another name.

## Reference Books

As well as the diary, mentioned above, you'll find a
personal reference book an invaluable aid. This can be
used for recording such details as how much coffee everyone
else drinks and whether they're paying their fair share.
You can use it for keeping a note of the boss's punctuality,
a useful ploy when you're being hauled over the carpet for
being late yourself. Names and telephone numbers need
somewhere to go, too; this little book is the obvious place.

There are certain general reference books that should be at
hand, too. *The Good Food Guide*, and the latest *Real Ale
Guide* are obviously essential, but others have their uses:

| | |
|---|---|
| Railway Timetables | Good for a laugh and handy for delaying unwelcome visitors. |
| Michelin Guides | For planning business trips abroad. |
| *The Sporting Life* | For keeping abreast of the market. |
| *The Times* | For the crossword. |
| *The Sun* | For keeping abreast of the market. |

## Essential Office Equipment

Apart from the kettle, the bottle opener and the corkscrew, which should be to the office what a lift is to a lift-shaft, the following articles are frequently found in well appointed offices (any office without the above mentioned can probably be done under the Health and Safety at Work Act);

| | |
|---|---|
| Stapling machine and staples | For Desk Archery |
| Perforator (punch) | For creative work with paper. |
| Scissors | For further creative work with paper; mending plugs; running repairs to work clothes. |
| Sellotape | For repairing window cracks; silencing office bores; repairing coffee cups; resealing confidential mail steamed open over kettle. |
| Ash tray | For feeding office cat; collecting beer money; drawing lots for any major decision (e.g. who buys first round). |
| Telex pads | For notes; Desk Archery; messages on the strange machine that rattles out messages from time to time. |
| Paper clips, rubber bands | For Desk Archery. |
| Blu-tac | For mounting page 3; for sticking under adversary's desk like old chewing gum; for plugging leaks in kettle, or anything else; for Desk Archery. |

## Dress and Grooming

Care should be taken over one's appearance at work.
The men should try to give the impression of genteel
poverty. Sharp suits, silk ties, Russell and Bromley
shoes, cashmere coats do nothing, if you want a rise,
except make your boss envious. Dress for the office
as you would if you were appearing in court in a
divorce case and wanted to dodge paying through the
nose. Hair, if you still have any, should be cared for
with an eye to the typing pool. If you're in the typing
pool it should be cared for with an eye to the Director
of Finance, or if he's beyond the pale, his son. If you
give as much attention dressing for the office as you
would to a party, fancy-dress or otherwise, you will
always be certain of gaining the right attention.

## Posture

Posture is never more important in the office than after lunch. The temptation to slump against the wall of the lift, clutching onto the ventilator grill, must be resisted at all costs; you never know who may be waiting to get in when the doors open on your floor. At your desk it's as well to sit as upright as you can, making sure that your head is perpendicular to your centre of gravity. When walking about the office, walk straight and positively until you're out of the door. If you're in doubt about making it in a straight line, try to go out with a friend who can steer you in the right direction.

## Office Communication and Correspondence

It can't all be left to machines and sometimes it can't be left to other people either. So when you're forced into putting pen to paper, or mouth to microphone remember the rules:

1. Don't use no double negatives.
2. Make each pronoun agree with their antecedent.
3. Join clauses good, like a conjunction should.
4. About them sentence fragments.
5. When dangling, watch your particles.
6. Verbs has to agree with their subject.
7. Just between you and I, case are important to.
8. Don't write run-on sentences they are hard to read.
9. Don't use commas, which aren't necessary.
10. Try to not oversplit infinitives.

WHEN IN DOUBT, SMILE
— IT ALWAYS MAKES PEOPLE
WONDER WHAT YOU'RE THINKING.

**Success is a matter
of luck — just ask
any failure!**

WHEN IN CHARGE, PONDER.
WHEN IN TROUBLE, DELEGATE

2B OR
NOT 2B....

Give more than they ask for.
More is less, but it looks like more.

A rolling stone
    angers his boss.

GENIUS IS 10% INSPIRATION
AND 50% CAPITAL GAINS.

...OR SHOULD
    I USE A BIRO?

# HOW TO SUCCEED IN BUSINESS
# BY TRYING DESPERATELY HARD

ROBBIN'S RULES OF MARKETING

1. Your share of the market is really lower than you think.
2. Never delay the end of a meeting or the beginning of a cocktail hour.
3. The combined market position goals of all competitors always totals at least 150 per cent.
4. The existence of a market does not always ensure the existence of a customer.
5. Strategies develop most easily from big backlogs.
6. Beware of alleged needs that have no real market.
7. The worth of a thing is what it will bring.
8. Low price and long shipment will win over high price and short shipment.
9. Umbrella pricing encourages noncompetitive costs.
10. The competition really can have lower prices.
11. If you can't get the whole job, settle for part of it.
12. The number of competitors never decline.
13. Secret negotiations are usually neither.
14. A good presentation has as many questions as answers.

15. If the customer wants vanilla, give him vanilla.
16. If the customer buys lunch, you've lost the order.
17. Unless constantly nurtured, nothing is as short-lived as a good customer.
18. No matter how good the deal, the customer is always sceptical.

1. To study a subject best, understand it thoroughly before you start.
2. Always keep a record of data. It indicates you've been working.
3. Always draw your curves, then plot the reading.
4. In case of doubt, make it sound convincing.
5. Experiments should be reproducible. They should all fail in the same way.
6. Do not believe in miracles. Rely on them.
7. If an experiment works, something has gone wrong.
8. No matter what result is anticipated, there will always be someone eager (a) to misinterpret it, (b) fake it, or (c) believe it happened to his own pet theory.
9. In any collection of data, the figure most obviously correct, beyond all need of checking, is the mistake.
   *Corollary 1:* No one whom you ask for help will see it.
   *Corollary 2:* Everyone who stops by with unsought advice will see it immediately.
10. Once a job is fouled up, anything done to improve it only makes it worse.
11. Science is truth – don't be misled by facts.

1. He who gets too big for his britches gets exposed in the end.
2. Staying afloat in management is easier if you don't make big waves.
3. The only people making money these days are the ones who sell computer paper.
4. If you don't have problems, you wouldn't need people around to help solve them. Conversely, if you didn't have people around, maybe you wouldn't have problems.
5. Nothing motivates a man more than to see his boss putting in an honest day's work.
6. Bosses are so busy delegating jobs, they have no time to do any work.
7. When someone else blows their horn, it sounds like a Cadillac. When *you* toot, it sounds like a Volkswagen.
8. People who mind their business succeed because they have so little competition.
9. You can tell some people aren't afraid of work by the way they fight it.

SPARK'S TEN RULES FOR THE PROJECT MANAGER

1. Strive to look tremendously important.
2. Attempt to be seen with important people.
3. Speak with authority; however, only expound on the obvious and proven facts.
4. Don't engage in arguments, but if cornered, ask an irrelevant question and lean back with a satisfied grin while your opponent tries to figure out what's going on – then quickly change the subject.
5. Listen intently while others are arguing the problem. Pounce on a trite statement and bury them with it.
6. If a subordinate asks you a pertinent question, look at him as if he had lost his senses. When he looks down, paraphrase the question back at him.
7. Obtain a brilliant assignment, but keep out of sight and out of the limelight.
8. Walk at a fast pace when out of the office – this keeps questions from subordinates and superiors at a minimum.
9. Always keep the office door closed. This puts visitors on the defensive and also makes it look as if you are always in an important conference.
10. Give all orders verbally. Never write anything down that might be used in evidence against you.

105

# DECISION MAKING

1) If you must make a decision, delay it.

2) If you can authorise someone else to avoid a decision, do so.

3) If you can form a committee, have them avoid a decision.

4) If you can otherwise avoid a decision, avoid it immediately.

THOSE WHO THINK THEY KNOW IT ALL UPSET THOSE OF US THAT DO!

Necessity is the mother of convention.

IT'S COMPANY POLICY —WORK HARD OR LOOK GOOD IN A TIGHT SWEATER!

The wages of sin vary considerably.

# HOW TO BE AN INTERNATIONAL EXECUTIVE

MASTER THE LANGUAGES OF INTERNATIONAL BUSINESS ...

THE BUSINESSMAN ABROAD: A MULTINATIONAL PHRASE BOOK

| | |
|---|---|
| à bientôt | just a drop |
| abito | some, a piece of |
| ab imo | it's his |
| achtung | I've got a sore mouth |
| actif | keen |
| action préférentielle | nepotism |
| à fond | source of money |
| ahorro | boss's personal assistant |
| aide de camp | gay p.a. |
| à la carte | served from the trolley |
| amende honorable | proper (decent) repair to clothing |
| analyse du chemin critique | how to get back to the office after 'business' lunch |

| | |
|---|---|
| Angebot | 'Please wait' |
| Anlage | 'Skol, please' |
| apenas | joy, pleasure (often the source of) |
| apéritif | dentures |
| artichaut | sneeze |
| Aussicht | domestic illness |
| Autofahrt | backfire |
| avant-garde | chastity belt |

| | |
|---|---|
| bagatelle | talkative woman |
| baroque | hiccup in cash flow |
| battre le pavé | thump the pavement |
| bénéfices d'exploitation | backhander |
| bien | French vegetable |
| billet | academic qualification |
| bord de la route | soliciting hitchhiker |
| brouhaha | French joy of cooking |
| Brottosozialprodukt | juvenile delinquent |

| | |
|---|---|
| ça ne fait rien | good weather |
| capuccino | small hat |
| cercle privé | lavatory seat |
| c'est magnifique | it's huge, enormous |
| château | French small talk |
| chômage | respect shown to boss |
| compota, compôte | left-overs |
| coq d'or | entry to Gents |
| cortège | weekend retreat |
| cum priviligio | he had the honour of her company |

| | |
|---|---|
| damnosa | inquisitive |
| déjeuner | to travel |
| déjâ vu | boo! |
| de mal en pis | 'Where's the …?' |

| | |
|---|---|
| déshabiller | to kick the habit |
| disponsibilités | passing the buck |
| Elite | match |
| émeraudes | piles |
| émigré | violent headache |
| émission d'actions gratuites | slush fund |

109

| | |
|---|---|
| en arrière | suppository |
| en gros | overweight |
| épices | business entertaining |
| esprit de corps | liquor served in service messes |
| extrados | more please |
| fabrication | annual report |
| faggotto | cigarette |
| farci | result of excessive stuffing with food |
| faux pas | don't do it |
| fiasco | Italian wine bottle |
| flèche | skin |
| (à) forte intensité de main | a bunch of fives |
| frais généraux | bonuses |
| fruits de mer | sea weed |
| gendarme | the strong arm of the law |
| gestion de stock | quality control (catering) |
| Gewinnspanne | aircraft tool |
| grand prix | boast |
| Grosshandel | clumsy |
| Gurke | pardon |
| hasta la vista | you have nice views |
| Haushalt | front door |
| heures supplementaires | overmanning in typing pool |
| homme d'affaires | busy man; gigolo |
| homo sapiens | consenting adult |
| hors concours | horse chestnut |
| hors de combat | camp followers |
| horloge | house of low repute |

| In toto | nail |
| infra dig | archaeologist |
| in statu pupillari | contact lens |
| inter alia | Italian internal flights |
| intermezzo | period between meals |
| in vino veritas | 'there is a worm in my wine' |

| jeu d'esprit | piss up |
| jus divinum | wine |
| karat | vegetable like an orange turnip |
| kip | chicken |
| kipper | chick |
| laissez-faire | secretary to whom job satisfaction has little to do with shorthand and typing |
| Lagerkontrolle | barman |
| lampone | raspberry |
| legato | foot |
| libido | bathroom fitting |
| libretto | type of sandal |
| lingua franca | laying it on the line |
| 'L'état c'est moi' | 'I am in a state' |
| lieu | (in lieu), engaged |
| Lockartikel | key |

| | |
|---|---|
| maladie | French distraction |
| mal de mer | battered baby |
| marge bénéficiaire | canteen cost-cutting propaganda |
| marché à terme | lift out of order |

| | |
|---|---|
| marque de fabrique | incontinence |
| matières brutes | industrial relations |
| ménage à trois | to share the burden |
| negligé | cause of distraction; careless |
| n'importe | trade barrier |
| noblesse oblige | it's too late to repent |
| non compos mentis | non-biodegradable |
| nota bene | potato |
| obiit | push off! |
| odium theologicum | incense |
| omphallus | large symbol |
| par excellence | professional golf handicap |
| pas de deux | father of twins |

| | |
|---|---|
| passé | the old man said |
| per annum | laxative |
| piano | shipping line |
| pis aller | gutter |
| pizzicato | Italian take-away |
| polonaise | hay fever |
| post-obitum | earth re-entry |
| presto | tight (shoe) |
| prévisions | canteen orders |

| | |
|---|---|
| quod erat demonstrandum | there are four mistakes |
| rentier | payment to landlord |
| sang froid | black pudding |
| savoir faire | to know 'a good thing' |
| semper paratus | once a parrot, always a parrot |
| son et lumière | 'boy, you're lit up!' |
| sotto voce | slurred speech |
| sub poena | (as above) under the piano |
| table d'hôte | hot dish |
| tant pis | Auntie's had too much |

| | |
|---|---|
| tartine | sweet little French waitress |
| terra cotta | clinophobia |
| terra firma | fear of business organizations |
| terra incognita | fear of the unknown |
| tertium quid | 3,000 new pence |
| tour de force | inspection |
| tour de main | palmistry |
| tout de suite | all the pudding |
| vidi, vici, veni | 'I saw, I conquered, I came'. See 'wanderlust' |
| vis-à-vis | to return the insult |
| voltarsi | leap-frog |

| | |
|---|---|
| Wanderlust | see: 'bord de la route' |
| Zweifellos | a couple of chaps |

And know who to call when you need them ...

Don't waste time wading through other directories only
to make dud calls. Go straight to the top and main-line
it where it counts! (Area codes not provided):

President Reagan Washington D.C. 456–2573
President Brehznev Moscow 206–25–11
Henry Ford Dearborn 322–3000
Euthanasia Education
 Council, Inc. New York 246–6962

Horoscopes New York 936–5950/6262
Salvation Army Alcohol
 and Drug Addiction
 Centre Sydney 272–2322
Ambulance Service Bangkok 13
Musée des Beaux Arts Beirut 2–52–85
NASA Washington D.C. 755–8364
Worldwide Rent-a-Car Sharjah 355547
Dial-an-angel Sydney 467–1511
Credit Suisse Zurich 215–1111
Oil Can Harry's Vancouver 683–7306
St. George Brewery Addis Ababa 47295
North Pizza Pantry Tehran 285765
International Casino Nairobi 56000

| | |
|---|---|
| Windsor Castle | Windsor 68286 |
| Playboy Enterprises Inc. | Chicago 751–8000 |
| Magistrate's Office | Soweto 825–1061 |
| Christian Dior | Paris 359–83–72 |
| Gucci | Los Angeles 278–3451 |
| Pinkerton's, Inc. | New York 285–4860 |
| Guyana Distilleries Ltd. | Georgetown 66171 |
| British Embassy | Ulan Bator 51033/4 |
| Dial-a-Girl | Johannesburg 23–9547 |
| Colt Fire-arms | Hartford 278–8550 |
| Gstaad Golf Course | Gstaad 42636 |
| Ministry of Education | Zomba 611 |
| 'La Poms' (hairdresser) | Auckland 65–777 |
| Air & Sea Rescue | Bahamas 2–3877 |
| Sony Corporation | Tokyo 448–2111 |
| Watergate | Washington D.C. 965–2300 |
| Raffles Hotel | Singapore 328041 |
| Cartier Inc. | New York 753–0111 |
| Comdates Computer Service | San Francisco 391–8181 |
| Warner Brothers Inc. | Burbank 845–6000 |
| Acropolis | Athens 3236–665 |
| Sunset Club | Lima 22–9874 |
| Texaco, Inc. | White Plains 253–4000 |
| Teatro alla Scala | Milan 8879 |
| Topkapi Palace | Istanbul 28–35–47 |
| Wayside Chapel Crisis Centre | Sydney 33–4251 |
| Committee for the Scientific Investigation of Claims of the Paranormal | Buffalo 837–0306 |

| | |
|---|---|
| Penthouse Club | Copenhagen 14–35–35 |
| Ting Li Kwan Restaurant | Peking 281–936 |
| The Raja of Perlis | Perlis 7552211 |
| Central Intelligence Agency | Washington D.C. 351–1100 |
| Omaha Grain Exchange | Omaha 341–6733 |
| Dubai Broadcasting | Dubai 470255 |
| Professional Rodeo Cowboys Association | Denver 455–3270 |
| Champagne J. Bollinger SA | Reims 50–12–34 |
| Kaziranga Wildlife Sanctuary | Kaziranga 3 |

SUCCESS IS MAKING MORE
MONEY TO PAY THE TAXES
YOU WOULDN'T HAVE TO PAY IF
YOU DIDN'T MAKE SO MUCH MONEY

off the top of the head
ideas are like dandruff
— small and flaky!

# MANY HANDS
## WANT LIGHT WORK

They are not long,
the Days of Whine and Rises.

Money isn't everything
— It isn't even enough!

THEY TOLD HIM THE JOB
COULDN'T BE DONE;

HE ROLLED UP HIS SLEEVES
AND SET TO IT.

HE TACKLED THE JOB
THAT COULDN'T BE DONE;

— AND HE COULDN'T DO IT!

# HOW TO LIVE ON YOUR SALARY

Be philosophic about it ... you can't.

## WHEN A MAN TELLS YOU HE GOT RICH THROUGH HARD WORK, ASK HIM WHOSE?

ON THEIR MEANNESS
(*With acknowledgement to J. Milton*)

When I consider how my time is spent,
Ere half my days, working fiddles on the side,
And that one talent for which so hard I tried,
Lodged with me useless, my hours hell bent
To appease therewith my bank manager and present
A black account, lest he return post chide,
Doth the top brass expect slave-labour, pay increases
   denied,
I fondly ask; but a memo to prevent
That murmur, soon replies, this firm doth not need
Either men's brains or their own gifts, who best
Bear our workload, they serve us best, their state
Is humble. Executives on a whim may speed
Away to bask by sun-drenched oceans on American
   Express:
But increments for you, for the upturn must await.

And you must accept that the size of your salary merely reflects the hours you work ...

OUR WORKING SCHEDULE

| | |
|---|---|
| Starting time | 9.00 am |
| Morning Coffee Break | 9.30–11.30 am |
| Lunch Hour | 12.00–2.00 pm |
| Afternoon Tea Break | 2.30–4.30 pm |
| Home Time | 5.00 pm |

The management has decided to introduce a more efficient and easily understood time-sheet. The time-sheet is designed for submission on a monthly basis but the firm has arranged for the data to be submitted at fortnightly intervals. In spite of the fact that data are submitted fortnightly, staff should complete time sheets each week.

NOTICE TO ALL EMPLOYEES

Some time between starting and quitting time, without infringing on lunch periods, coffee breaks, rest periods, storytelling, ticket-selling, holiday planning, and the rehashing of yesterday's TV programme, we ask that each employee try to find some time for a work break.
This may seem radical, but it might aid steady employment, assure regular pay checks.

Spielman Chevrolet Company of New York.


NOTICE TO ALL EMPLOYEES

In view of the recently adopted 'personal productivity remuneration and increment contract' (PPRIC) you are reminded that your salary is your personal business, and should not be disclosed to anyone. Employees found revealing their PPRICs to other member of staff will be dealt with according to the agreed disciplinary procedure.

# He who ploughs a straight furrow is probably in a rut

SOME PEOPLE ARE STILL WILLING TO DO AN HONEST DAY'S WORK, BUT THEY WANT A WEEK'S PAY FOR IT!

## If you try You might If you don't You won't!

IF YOU CAN'T SEE THE BRIGHT SIDE — POLISH THE DULL SIDE

In this company all employees are completely dispensible — except when they want a day off.

The difference between this firm and a cactus plant is that the plant has the pricks on the outside

# HOW TO ENJOY
# THE OFFICE PARTY

The chances are that something of major importance will be happening at 9.00 am the morning after the binge – a board meeting; a crucial sales meeting; the signing of the contract. Whatever it is you're never in shape for it. Worse still, you've got to face the rest of the office. But if you can pull yourself together, retrieve your head and clear it, when everyone else is wishing they'd quietly disposed of theirs, you could score a few valuable status points. So the morning after should be spent wisely. A couple of hours can work miracles.

HANGOVER TIMETABLE

| | |
|---|---|
| 6.50 am. | Open eyes |
| 6.55 am. | Focus eyes |
| 7.00 am. | Reach for radio-alarm |
| 7.01 am. | Turn off radio |
| 7.10 am. | Rise and stagger to bathroom |

| | |
|---|---|
| 7.15 am. | Clean teeth thoroughly |
| 7.20 am. | Drink as much water as you can – then drink some more |
| 7.30 am. | Drink glass of water with two seltzers |
| 7.32 am. | Take shower, or bath if you can't stand up |
| 7.50 am. | Shave |
| 7.55 am. | Drink more water and clean teeth again |
| 8.00 am. | Breakfast – porridge with salt and cream; cereals with plenty of milk and soft brown sugar; dry toast; scrambled eggs; whatever you reckon you can keep down. PLUS lots of hot, sweet tea or coffee. |

| 8.20 am. | Leave table and prepare morning's treat (you need something to pep you up by now) |
|---|---|
| 8.25 am. | Morning treat – whichever of the following you fancy, or can manage: |

8.25 am. Morning treat – whichever of the following you fancy, or can manage:

Sparkling wine (Champagne if you can afford it and don't mind the waste)
Fresh orange juice
Mixed in proportions of three to one
*or,*
2 tablespoons of scotch
3 tablespoons double cream
3 tablespoons honey
Shake (or stir if you can't take the noise) with ice and sip soothingly
*or,*
1 tablespoon of lemon juice
1 tablespoon of Worcestershire sauce
6 drops Tabasco
1 measure of Vodka (according to quantity of tomato juice)
Stir with ice

8.30 am. Leave for work with thermos of hot, sweet beverage to drink in private before facing the office

8.55 am. Clean teeth once more; wash face in cold water; drink contents of thermos; comb hair and straighten tie.

9.00 am. SOCK IT TO 'EM, BABY!

## A WORKERS' PRAYER

Our gaffer who art a heathen,
Broken be thy name.
Thy receiver come.
Thy ruin done from Perth as far as Devon.
But give us till then our weekly bread.
And forgive us our secondary picketing,
As we forgive them that blackleg against us.
And lead us not into arbitration;
But deliver the gravy:
For thine is the Greek island,
The Rolls and the mistress,
Paid for by the sweat of
Our men.